GLEN ROCK PUBLIC LIBRARY
GLEN ROCK, N J 07452

Twenty
INVENTORS

Jacqueline Dineen

Illustrated by Gary Rees

MARSHALL CAVENDISH
New York, London, Toronto

Editor: Deborah Elliott
Consultant Editor: Maggi McCormick

Reference Edition published 1988

© Marshall Cavendish Limited 1988
© Wayland (Publishers) Limited 1988

Published by Marshall Cavendish Corporation
147 West Merrick Road
Freeport
Long Island
N.Y. 11520

Library of Congress Cataloging in Publication Data

Dineen, Jacqueline.
    Twenty inventors / Jacqueline Dineen.
       p. cm. — (Twenty names)
   Bibliography: p.
   Includes index.
   Summary: A collection of twenty brief biographies of inventors
   ISBN 0-86307-969-5 : $12.95
    1. Inventors-Biography-Juvenile literature. [1. Inventors.]
I. Title. II. Title: 20 inventors III. Series.
T39. D56 1988
809. 2'2—dc19
[B]
[920]   88-20992
                                      CIP
                                       AC

All rights reserved. No part of this book may be reproduced or utilized in
any form by any means electronic or mechanical, including photocopying,
recording, or by information storage and retnieval system, without
permission from the copyright holder.

Printed in Italy by G. Canale & C. S.p.A. - Turin.

Contents

Inventors and inventions　　　　　4
 1 Archimedes　　　　　　　　　 6
 2 Johann Gutenberg　　　　　　 8
 3 Richard Arkwright　　　　　　10
 4 James Watt　　　　　　　　　12
 5 George Stephenson　　　　　　14
 6 Louis Braille　　　　　　　　　16
 7 Christopher Sholes　　　　　　18
 8 Gottlieb Daimler　　　　　　　20
 9 John Dunlop　　　　　　　　　22
10 Alexander Graham Bell　　　　24
11 Thomas Alva Edison　　　　　26
12 Marie Curie　　　　　　　　　28
13 Wilbur and Orville Wright　　 30
14 Guglielmo Marconi　　　　　　32
15 John Logie Baird　　　　　　　34
16 Caresse Crosby　　　　　　　36
17 Ladislao Biro　　　　　　　　38
18 Frank Whittle　　　　　　　　40
19 Wernher von Braun　　　　　 42
20 Rosalind Franklin　　　　　　44
Glossary　　　　　　　　　　　　46
Further reading　　　　　　　　　46
Index　　　　　　　　　　　　　47

Inventors and inventions

Every single tool that people use had to be invented first. The first people on earth had nothing but the animals, plants and minerals around them. They had to invent simple tools so they could hunt for food. They made cooking vessels and utensils, and invented ways of making clothes to keep themselves warm.

When people began to settle down in communities, their inventions became more sophisticated. They invented tools for farming the land and methods of taking water to their crops. They thought of ways to build houses and began to use available minerals to make ornaments and jewelry.

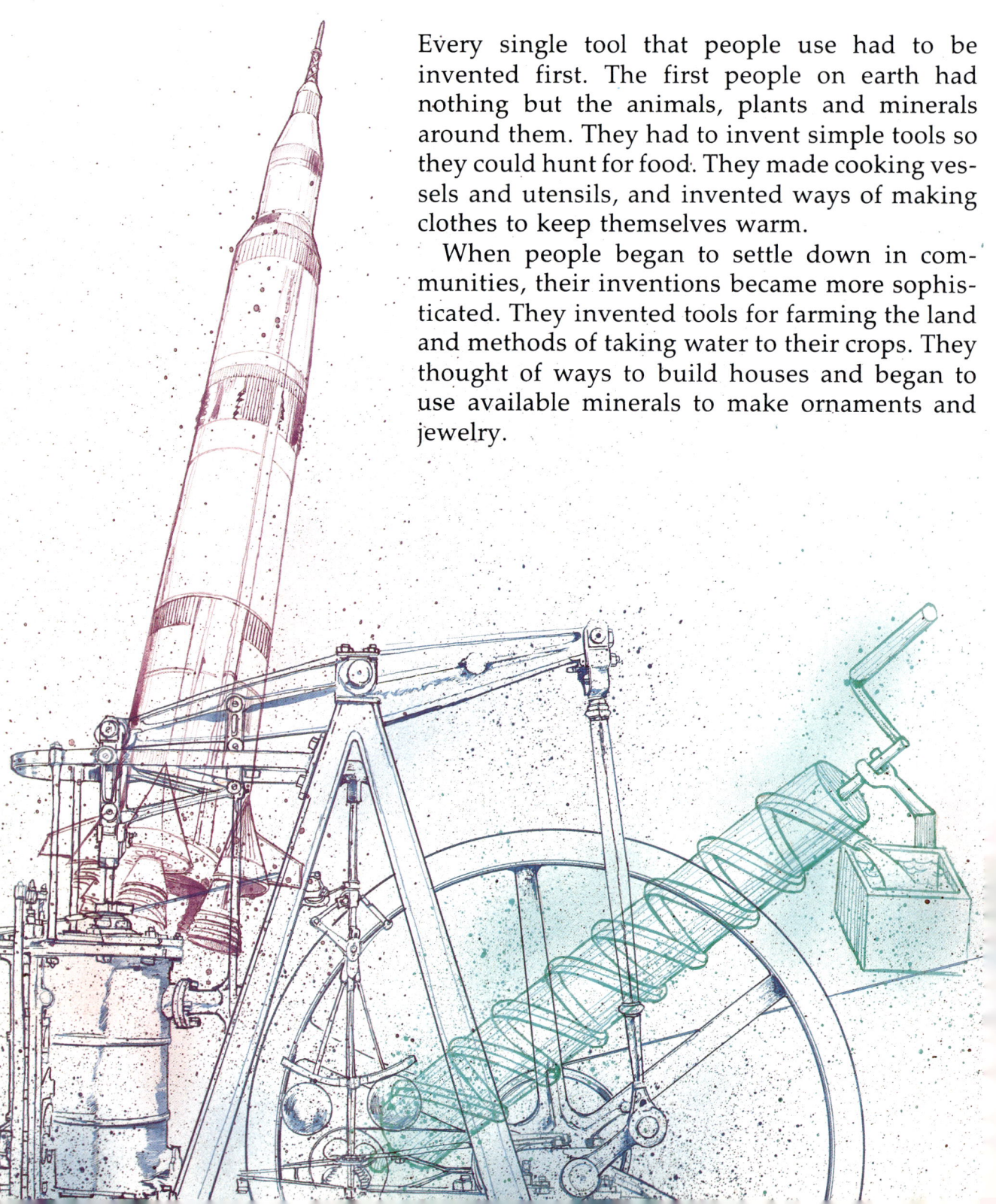

When you think of the thousands of years that have passed and the world we live in today, you can see that there have been millions of inventions since those early days.

In this book, we shall look at a few of the people whose inventions have changed our lives very dramatically, such as Alexander Graham Bell's telephone, James Watt's steam engine and Johann Gutenberg's printing press. Before this century, very few women had the opportunities that were available to men in the fields of science and invention. However, women such as Rosalind Franklin, whose studies contributed to the discovery of DNA, are now proving their skills and abilities in these fields alongside male colleagues. Most inventions in the twentieth century are made by teams and not by individuals.

1
Archimedes

Archimedes was the most brilliant inventor and mathematician of the ancient world. As a young man, he studied math at a school in Alexandria founded by the Greek mathematician, Euclid. When he returned to Syracuse, Archimedes began to solve geometry problems. He was the first person to experiment with levers for lifting heavy objects. He is supposed to have said that he could move the earth if he only had somewhere to rest a lever!

Archimedes' most famous invention was a device for lifting water. He designed it to drain water from a flooded ship. A large screw was rotated inside a wooden cylinder. The water was drawn up the screw and came out at the top of the cylinder. This device, called the Archimedes Screw, is still used today in some countries of the world. For example, farmers along the banks of the River Nile in Egypt use it for lifting river water to irrigate their land.

In about 213 BC, Archimedes made the discovery that if an object is put into a full vessel of water, the volume of the water which overflows is equal to the volume of the object. This is known as Archimedes' Principle.

In 215 BC, the Romans attacked Syracuse. There are many legends about the war machines which Archimedes invented to help his friend, King Hieron, keep the Romans at bay. According to one legend, he is said to have designed huge mirrors which used the sun's rays to set fire to the Roman ships. Another legend tells of cranes which grabbed the ships and overturned them, and giant catapults which hurled stones at the Romans.

Despite Archimedes' efforts, Syracuse was defeated by the Romans in 212 BC, and he was killed. This angered the Roman general, Marcellus, who had wanted Archimedes' life to be spared. A mathematical genius had been lost.

c. 287 BC born in Syracuse on the island of Sicily
215 BC Romans invade Syracuse; invents war machines for King Hieron
c. 213 BC discovery of Archimedes' Principle
212 BC killed by Roman soldier at Syracuse

Below *Archimedes using some of his inventions to help King Hieron protect Syracuse from the Roman attack in 215 BC.*

2
Johann Gutenberg

Imagine a world without books, newspapers, magazines and all the other printed material we take for granted today. People had none of these things before Johann Gutenberg invented the printing press in the fifteenth century. Although there were a few books available at that time, most people did not have access to them. Each book was handwritten by monks, and it took months to produce a single copy. The books they produced were so rare and precious that they were locked away in monastery libraries.

Gutenberg was born in the German town of Mainz, where his father was the Master of the Mint. The young boy was fascinated by the way the goldsmiths stamped letters and figures onto coins. Eventually, he became a skilled metal-worker himself.

Gutenberg was also interested in the handwritten books in the monastery library. He would spend hours poring over them and watching the monks laboriously copying the scripts. As he

c. 1397 born in Mainz, Germany
1428 moves to Strasbourg and begins to experiment with printing equipment
1448 returns to Mainz and tries to borrow money for his work
1450 forms partnership with Johann Fust and begins to set up printing press
1456 prints 300 copies of the 1,282 page *Gutenberg Bible*
1468 dies in Mainz

Right *In 1456, Gutenberg's printing press was used to produce copies of the Bible.*

8

watched, an idea came to him. Could a metalwork process be used to produce words on a page? Gutenberg's idea was to cut the letters of the alphabet on individual blocks of metal which could then be moved around to form words. He invented a printing press in which metal letters were fitted into a frame to make up the words on a page.

Gutenberg was a poor man, and he needed money to develop his idea. Therefore, he agreed to a proposal put to him by a cunning lawyer named Johann Fust. Fust offered to pay for the printing press, inks and papers Gutenberg needed if he could become Gutenberg's partner.

In 1456, Fust printed 300 copies of the famous *Gutenberg Bible*. This was the beginning of book publishing and should have made Gutenberg rich and famous. But Fust was greedy, and decided to get rid of his partner. He demanded his money back. Gutenberg could not pay, so Fust seized his equipment and took over the business. Gutenberg did not earn any money from his invention and died penniless twelve years later.

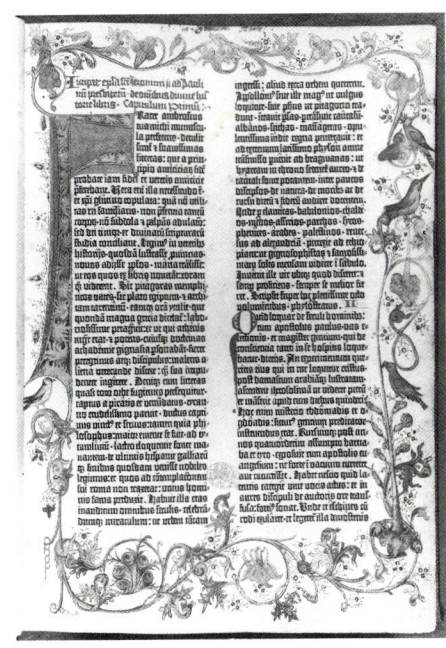

Above *A page from the Gutenberg Bible.*

3
Richard Arkwright

The craft of spinning – twisting threads into a long yarn – is thousands of years old. Until the Middle Ages, a spinner used two sticks, called a distaff and a spindle, for drawing out the threads and twisting them into yarn. Then, spinning wheels were introduced, and, in about 1767, James Hargreaves invented the spinning jenny. This hand-operated machine made spinning faster, but did not produce a very strong thread.

Richard Arkwright was born in Lancashire in England. He turned spinning from a cottage craft into a large-scale industry when he invented his water-powered spinning frame in 1769. Arkwright was one of seven children, and when he was ten years old, he became an apprentice in a barbershop. Here, he learned to make hair dyes and wigs, which he sold in nearby towns and villages.

Below *Richard Arkwright tries to protect his spinning mill from spinners and weavers who were afraid that the new machine would put them out of work.*

As he traveled around, Arkwright would stop to watch the local cotton weavers at work. He noticed that they used cotton for the weft (crosswise) threads, but Irish linen for the warp (lengthwise) threads. The weavers explained that spinners could not produce cotton thread which was fine and strong enough for the warp. The problem interested Arkwright greatly, so he worked out an idea for a spinning frame driven by a water wheel. The cotton passed between two sets of rollers moving at different speeds and was then drawn out into fine, strong threads. Spindles twisted the threads into yarn and wound it onto bobbins.

In 1771, Arkwright opened his first spinning mill in Derbyshire. At first, people were suspicious. The spinners and weavers thought the new machinery would put them out of a job, and the cotton manufacturers thought it would be too expensive. But Arkwright continued to improve his machines, and more manufacturers began to use them. He lived to see his home county of Lancashire become the center of the world's cotton trade.

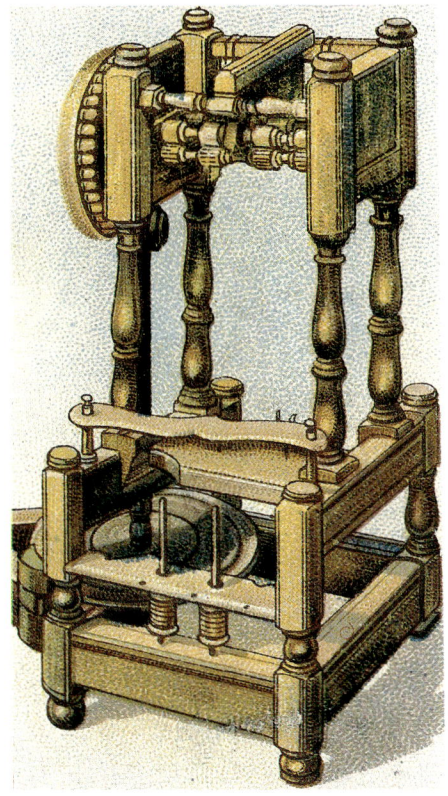

Above *Arkwright invented the water-powered spinning frame in 1769.*

Below left *The spinning machine invented by Arkwright in 1767.*

1732	born in Preston, Lancashire, England
1742	begins work in a barbershop
1769	invents the first water-powered spinning frame
1771	first spinning mill opens in Cromford, Derbyshire, England
1792	dies in Cromford

4
James Watt

In 1712, a hardware dealer named Thomas Newcomen, from Devonshire in England, invented a steam engine for pumping water out of tin and coal mines. Newcomen received little recognition for his invention, but, for the next fifty years, it was the only method of keeping mines free of water.

James Watt was the son of a merchant from Greenock in Scotland. He trained as a mathematical instrument maker, and in 1757, he set up a shop at Glasgow University. In 1763, Watt was asked to mend a model of a Newcomen engine which belonged to the university. He realized that the engine had several faults and decided to build a better one.

Below *James Watt modified Newcomen's steam engine so that it would turn a wheel and drive machinery in factories and mills.*

The main problem with the Newcomen engine was that the cylinder was alternately heated to a high temperature and then cooled to condense the steam. The engine, therefore, used a great deal of coal and was expensive to run. Watt designed an engine with a separate condenser, which meant that the cylinder could be kept hot all the time. This proved much more economical.

In 1774, Watt formed a partnership with a Birmingham manufacturer, Matthew Boulton. The two men became famous for their engines. Until 1781, the engines could only drive a shaft backward and forward for pumping. Then Watt invented a steam engine which drove a wheel in a rotating movement. This was a great step forward, and Watt's engines were soon being used to drive machinery in factories and mills.

Before the age of steam, horses were used to drive mill machinery. Watt introduced the term "horsepower" to measure the rate at which his engines worked. He calculated the performance of an average horse and compared this output with the power of his engines. The unit "horsepower" is still used today.

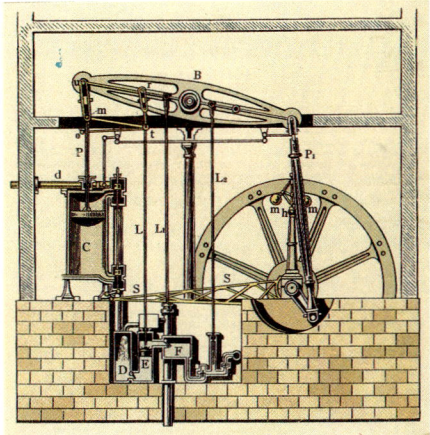

Above *A diagram showing Watt's steam engine.*

1736	born at Greenock, Scotland
1754	trains as a mathematical instrument maker
1765	invents a steam engine with a separate condenser
1774	forms a partnership with Matthew Boulton and moves to Birmingham, England
1781	invents an engine which drives a wheel in a rotating movement
1783	builds new engine and introduces the unit, "horsepower"
1819	dies at Heathfield, near Birmingham

Left *Young James Watt experimenting with steam.*

5
George Stephenson

As a boy growing up in eighteenth-century England, George Stephenson was fascinated by the steam engine at the coal mine where his father worked. In those days, steam engines were used to haul trucks along rails with chains, or to pump water out of the mines. Stephenson's father was in charge of the engine, and, when he was fourteen, the boy went to work with him. Stephenson had never been to school, but he longed to be an engineer. He spent all his spare time studying engines, and went to night school to learn to read and write.

In 1804, a Cornish engineer named Richard Trevithick designed a locomotive on wheels. Unfortunately, it was not a success. Stephenson resolved that he would build a better one. In 1814, he built a steam locomotive which could pull cars of coal from the mines to the port. It could haul about eight wagons holding 30 tons of coal at about 4½ mph.

1781	born near Newcastle-upon-Tyne, England
1814	builds his first locomotive
1821	begins the Stockton to Darlington railway
1825	*Locomotion* makes the first journey on the new line
1829	*Rocket* wins speed trials on the new Liverpool to Manchester line
1830	new line is opened
1848	dies in Cheltenham, Gloucestershire, England

In 1821, Stephenson and his son Robert began to build the first stretch of public railroad in England, between Stockton and Darlington. It was opened on September 27, 1825; and Stephenson's engine, *Locomotion*, pulled the world's first freight train along it. More than 400 people scrambled into the cars for the journey.

The Stephensons were asked to build another stretch of line between Manchester and Liverpool. In 1829, speed tests were held to choose a locomotive for the new line. George and Robert Stephenson's new engine, *Rocket*, pulled a train at 30 mph and won the trials.

The new line was opened in 1830. From then on, the rail network began to spread between all the big towns in England, and soon railroads were being built across most of the world's continents. The poor boy with no schooling had become the world's leading railroad engineer.

The Stephensons' engine Rocket *wins speed trials for the new railway between Manchester and Liverpool.*

6
Louis Braille

Today, blind people can read quickly and easily from books printed in Braille. They can work at many jobs using special machinery such as Braille typewriters. However, before Louis Braille invented his alphabet of raised dots, blind people were treated as outcasts. His invention opened up a new world for them.

Louis Braille was born in northern France. He was blinded when he was three years old. His father was a saddle maker, and the little boy loved to watch him work. One day, Louis crept into the workshop and tried to cut some leather by himself. The sharp knife slipped and stabbed him in the left eye. Both his eyes became infected, and, within a few months, he was blind.

When he was ten, Louis was sent to the National Institute for Blind Youth in Paris. There, children read from books with large raised letters,

1809	born in Coupvray, France
1812	blinded in father's workshop
1819	goes to the National Institute for Blind Youth in Paris, France
1824	begins to adapt Captain Barbier's system of "night writing"
1826	becomes a teacher of the blind
1829	Braille alphabet is introduced
1852	dies of tuberculosis at the Institute in Paris

which were heavy and difficult to use. Louis decided to invent a special alphabet with tiny symbols which would be easier to read.

In 1824, an army officer, Captain Charles Barbier, visited the Institute to demonstrate "night writing." This was a system of raised dots which he had invented for passing messages on a dark battlefield. Braille adopted this idea for his alphabet. He used six dots and worked out different patterns for all the letters and punctuation marks.

In 1826, Braille became a teacher at the Institute, where he remained for the rest of his life. His alphabet was first used at the Institute in 1829, but it was not known to the rest of the world until 1868, when a blind Englishman, Dr. Armitage, discovered it and began publishing books in Braille. In 1932, it was adopted as the main alphabet for the blind, and it is now widely used all over the world.

Below *Louis Braille was blinded at the age of three in an accident with his father's saddling knife.*
Left *He went on to invent an alphabet of raised dots for the blind.*

7
Christopher Sholes

Several people had attempted to design a typing machine before Christopher Sholes invented the first practical typewriter in 1867. In 1714, an English engineer, Henry Miller, patented a machine, but never manufactured it. William Burt, a blacksmith from Detroit, Michigan, made a clumsy wooden machine called a typographer in 1829. It was fitted with lead type from the local newspaper office. Other inventors came up with different ideas over the next forty years. Most of them tried to design machines which produced raised letters that blind people could read. No one thought of inventing a machine for "typing" business letters.

Christopher Sholes was the editor of a newspaper in Milwaukee, Wisconsin. He had an idea for a "letter printing machine," as he called it; and in 1864, he decided to leave his job and work on his invention. He found two partners, Carlos

1819	born Mooresburg, Pennsylvania
1864	leaves job as a newspaper editor to work on "letter printing machine"
1867	designs first practical typewriter
1868	patents his invention
1872	tries to market the typewriters
1873	sells invention to the Remington Small Arms Company
1890	dies in Milwaukee, Wisconsin

Right *Sholes' typewriters were used in offices and soon created jobs for many people.*

Glidden and Samuel Soulé; and, by 1867, they had designed their typewriter. They patented it in 1868. Modern typewriters are based on this machine, and the keyboard layout has changed very little since Sholes designed it. The first machine had several disadvantages, however. It printed everything in capital letters, and the operator could not see what he or she was typing because the paper was hidden by the carriage. Even so, it was a big improvement on earlier ideas.

Sholes began to make the typewriters in 1872, but he found it difficult to sell them. The following year, he sold his invention to the Remington Small Arms Company, who began to manufacture the machines.

Typewriters quickly became popular. Businesses began to use them; this created more jobs for women – lady typewriters, as the early typists were called. Mark Twain was the first author to buy a typewriter. He typed the manuscript for *Life on the Mississippi* on a Model 1 Remington in 1883.

Above *A model of an early typewriter.*

8
Gottlieb Daimler

Karl Benz is recognized as the father of the motor industry because he invented the first practical automobile. But the first successful gasoline-driven internal combustion engine was pioneered by another German, Gottlieb Daimler.

In 1862, a Belgian engineer, Etienne Lenoir, fitted an internal combustion engine driven by natural gas to a "horseless carriage." The vehicle had large wheels and did look very much like a carriage without a horse. But it was unwieldy, and the engine lacked power. Daimler knew Lenoir and was interested in his engine. It was suitable for driving factory machinery, but Daimler did not believe it was the answer for transport.

In 1872, Daimler became a factory manager for a German designer of gas engines, Nikolaus Otto. Otto asked Daimler to find out whether or not

Below *Daimler's revolutionary four-wheeled "horseless carriage" amazed many people when it first appeared on the roads in the 1880s.*

petroleum could be used as a fuel instead of natural gas. Daimler saw the possibilities of this idea. In 1882, he left Otto to set up his own company in his hometown of Cannstatt, in Germany, and began to develop his gasoline engine.

In 1885, Daimler fitted his first gasoline engine to a large bicycle. This was the ancestor of the modern motorcycle. In 1886, he produced a four-wheeled "horseless carriage," which had a top speed of 10 mph. The following year, he founded the Daimler Motor Company, which built the first Mercedes in 1901. The car was named after the baby daughter of Daimler's financial backer, Emil Jellinek.

Meanwhile, Karl Benz had designed the first practical car in 1885, and, by 1895, his cars were being manufactured in large numbers at his factory in Mannheim. The two men never met, but twenty-six years after Daimler's death, the two companies joined forces and began to manufacture the famous Mercedes-Benz.

Above *One of the original Daimler motor cars, invented in 1886.*

1834	born in Schorndorf, Germany
1860	visits Etienne Lenoir's factory in Paris
1872	becomes factory manager for Nikolaus Otto at Deutz, Germany
1882	leaves Otto to work on his gasoline engine
1885	fits engine to bicycle
1886	produces first gasoline-driven "horseless carriage"
1887	forms the Daimler Motor Company to make engines
1889	designs new two-cylinder engine which is much more powerful than its rivals
1900	dies in Cannstatt, Germany

9
John Dunlop

The first tires were made of iron and, as you can imagine, they gave a noisy and bumpy ride! Iron tires were used until the middle of the nineteenth century, when the rubber industry began. In 1846, an English rubber manufacturer, Thomas Hancock, made the first solid rubber tires, which were fitted to carriages and to bicycles. They were quieter than iron tires, but vehicles still bumped along the rough roads.

In 1845, a Scottish engineer, Robert William Thomson, designed the first "pneumatic" tire. It had a canvas cover and a rubber inner tube which was filled with air. But Thomson did not develop his invention, and it was soon forgotten.

Forty-five years later, John Dunlop invented the pneumatic tire we know today. Dunlop was

Right *A cross-section of a Dunlop tire.*

Far right *John Dunlop invented tires with air-filled inner tubes to make riding a bicycle much less bumpy.*

a Scottish veterinarian who was working in Belfast, Northern Ireland. One day in 1887, he bought his nine-year-old son, John, a tricycle with solid rubber tires. The little boy grumbled that it was bumpy riding along the cobbled streets. Dunlop thought about this problem, and in 1888, he made some tires with air-filled inner tubes. The outer covers were made of canvas, and the tires had rubber treads. Dunlop attached his tires to the wheel rims with a rubber solution so they were hard to get off. By 1890, however, the modern method had been introduced. The edges of the tire fitted inside a rim on the wheel. When it was full of air, the tire stayed firmly in place.

Dunlop patented his invention in 1888, and a Belfast company began to make the tires in 1890. This company later became the Dunlop Rubber Company. They made tires for bicycles and later for automobiles. By the early twentieth century, solid tires were a thing of the past.

1840 born in Dreghorn, Scotland
1888 makes pneumatic tires for son's tricycle; patents his invention
1890 sells patent to a Belfast company, but keeps some shares; the company manufactures the tires and later becomes the Dunlop Rubber Company
1921 dies in Dublin, Ireland

10
Alexander Graham Bell

Today, you can pick up a telephone and speak to someone almost anywhere in the world. Before the invention of the telephone in 1876, people had to send telegrams, write letters or visit each other when they wanted to communicate.

The telephone was invented by Alexander Graham Bell, a teacher of the deaf. Bell grew up in Scotland, but, when he was twenty-three, he contracted tuberculosis, and his family emigrated to Canada, where the climate was drier. He later moved to Boston, Massachusetts, where he continued to teach deaf children to speak. His interest in speech sounds gave him the idea that, somehow, speech could be sent along a wire. Bell knew that sound waves cause vibrations in the eardrum, and that this is what makes it possible for people to hear. He decided to make an electrical

Right *Bell and Thomas Watson had the first ever telephone conversation in 1875. Bell's invention transmitted sound using vibrating discs.*

24

transmitter with a vibrating disk which would pick up sound waves in the same way as the eardrum. This transmitter would be linked by wire to a receiver which also contained a vibrating disk. Sound vibrations would pass along the wire to the receiver, which would convert them back into words.

Bell and a young mechanic, Thomas Watson, worked for two years to make a successful transmitter. One evening in 1875, Bell set up the transmitter in his bedroom and spoke into it. Watson, holding the receiver in another room, heard him. The telephone had been invented!

Bell improved his equipment and transmitted telephone calls over longer distances. At first, people were afraid of voices coming to them over wires. They gradually got used to the idea, and the telephone system began to develop into the vast network we have today.

Above *Alexander Graham Bell, in the lecture hall of Boston University, uses a telephone to communicate with his friend in the basement.*

1847	born in Edinburgh, Scotland
1866	becomes a teacher of deaf children
1870	family emigrates to Canada
1875	first successful telephone transmission between two rooms
1876	first long-distance call between Brantford and Paris, Canada, 70 mi apart
1892	opens New York to Chicago telephone line
1922	dies in Nova Scotia, Canada

11
Thomas Alva Edison

The nineteenth century saw many changes in people's lives. It was a great age for inventors, and one of the most famous was Thomas Alva Edison. Most inventors were content with one or two inspirations in a lifetime, but Edison patented about 1,300 inventions, including the electric light and the phonograph.

In 1831, an English scientist named Michael Faraday found a way to produce electricity. Thirty-nine years later, Edison, then only seventeen, studied Faraday's work and invented an electric telegraph transmitter which could send out four messages at one time.

He moved to New York, where he invented new transmitting machinery for the Gold Indicator Company. He was paid $40,000 for his machine, and with the money, he set up a workshop in Newark, New Jersey. In 1876, he opened a factory at Menlo Park, near New York City. The following year, Edison invented the phonograph. Recordings were made on a metal cylinder and played back by a needle running through grooves.

1847	born in Milan, Ohio
1864	works for Western Union Telegraph Company; invents transmitter which can send four messages at once
1869	invents new machinery for the Gold Indicator Company, New York
1876	opens factory at Menlo Park, New York
1877	invents the phonograph
1878	forms Edison Electric Light Company
1880	first "illumination display"
1882	New York lit by electricity
1883	joins with British inventor, Joseph Swan, to form the Edison and Swan United Electric Company in London, England
1931	dies at West Orange, New Jersey

At this time, streets and buildings were lit by gas lamps. Edison's main ambition was to give the world electric light. In 1878, he formed the Edison Electric Light Company and began work. His first task was to make a light bulb. He discovered that if an electric current is passed through a thin thread, or filament, of carbon, the carbon becomes white hot and gives off a bright light. He knew that the filament would get too hot if it was fanned by the air, so he enclosed it in a sealed glass bulb from which the air had been removed.

In 1880, to everyone's excitement, Edison gave his first "illumination display" at Menlo Park. Not long after, New York became the first city to be lit by electricity. Edison continued to work on new inventions until just before his death at the age of eighty-four.

Above *Edison listens to a recording on his phonograph.*

Below *Edison working on the light bulb, just one of his 1,300 inventions.*

12
Marie Curie

As a young girl in Warsaw, Marie Sklodovska dreamed of becoming a great scientist. Her father, a science teacher, was too poor to help her, so Marie worked and saved until she could afford to go to the Sorbonne in Paris. Every night, when her lectures at the university were over, Marie studied in the freezing room which she rented. She was so poor that she nearly starved, but she achieved her ambition and gained honor degrees in physics and mathematics. She became the world's first great woman scientist.

In 1895, Marie married another scientist, Pierre Curie, and they began to work together. The French scientist, Antoine Becquerel, had already discovered that the mineral uranium gave off rays which could penetrate solid objects. Marie called this strange energy "radioactivity" and decided to investigate it further. Uranium came from an

1867 born in Warsaw, Poland
1891 begins studies at the Sorbonne, Paris
1895 marries Pierre Curie
1898 discovers polonium and radium in pitchblende
1902 extracts radium from pitchblende
1903 the Curies awarded the Nobel Prize for physics
1906 Pierre Curie killed
1911 wins Nobel Prize for chemistry
1914 Institute of Radium established in Paris; put in charge of radioactivity section
1934 dies in Paris

ore called pitchblende. Marie tested pitchblende and was astonished to find that it was more radioactive than the uranium. She realized that it must contain another radioactive element – one that no one had yet discovered.

Marie and Pierre began their work to find the radioactive elements. They did not have a real laboratory and had to work in a cold, leaking shed. At last, they discovered two new elements, which they named polonium and radium. They spent four more years trying to extract radium from pitchblende. They found that its powerful rays could heal wounds. Further tests showed that radium rays could cure diseased cells and destroy some cancerous tumors.

In 1906, Pierre was killed in a street accident. Marie was heartbroken; but, for the rest of her life, she continued the work they had started together. Her discoveries made a vital contribution to modern medicine and to the battle against cancer.

Above *The Curies at work in their laboratory.*

Left *Marie and Pierre Curie investigating radioactivity. Their discoveries led to great advances in the treatment of cancer.*

13
Wilbur and Orville Wright

People have always wanted to fly like birds, though their first efforts ended in disaster. They strapped on artificial wings and flapped their arms, but unfortunately, they all fell to the ground. The first success in flying came in 1783, when the Montgolfier brothers flew over Paris in a hot-air balloon. Then, in 1896, a German called Otto Lilienthal built a glider which stayed in the air for a few seconds.

The internal combustion engine (see page 20) made longer flights possible because it had the power to keep a heavy machine in the air. The first airplane was built in 1903 by two brothers, Wilbur and Orville Wright. The brothers had a bicycle repair shop in Dayton, Ohio, but their real ambition was build a flying machine powered by an engine. First, they fitted a bicycle with wings and an engine. Then, they experimented with gliders. In 1903, they built the *Flyer*, a biplane driven by a twelve-horsepower engine. On December 17, 1903, Orville took off

1867 Wilbur born in Dayton, Ohio
1871 Orville born in Dayton
1892 open bicycle repair shop in Dayton
1900 begin to experiment with gliders
1903 build the first *Flyer*
Orville makes the first flight
1908 Orville demonstrates the new *Flyer* in America. He is airborne for 1¼ hours.
Wilbur demonstrates another *Flyer* in France and remains in the air for 2 hours 20 minutes
1909 asked to build military planes
set up aircraft factory and flying school in Dayton
1912 Wilbur dies of typhoid fever in Millville, Indiana
1948 Orville dies in Dayton

in the *Flyer* from Kill Devil Hill, Kitty Hawk, in North Carolina. The plane reached a height of 10 ft and stayed in the air for 12 seconds. The brothers made three more flights that day. The longest one lasted 59 seconds and the plane flew about 300 yds. The brothers were triumphant, but the newspapers did not believe them and ignored their achievements.

The Wrights began to build more powerful planes. In 1908, Wilbur flew their new *Flyer* at Le Mans in France, and Orville demonstrated another *Flyer* to the American War Department. In 1909, the Wright brothers were asked to build the world's first military planes. At last, people had acknowledged that powered and controlled flight for humans was a reality.

Below *The Wright brothers' Flyer achieved the first engine-powered flight at Kitty Hawk, North Carolina, on December 17, 1903.*

14
Guglielmo Marconi

In 1894, a young Italian named Guglielmo Marconi read a newspaper article about magnetic waves of electricity which traveled through space at about 187,500 miles a second. Marconi felt sure that these "wireless" waves (or radio waves, as they are called today) could be used in some way. He rigged up a workshop in the attic of his parents' villa near Bologna and began to experiment. First, he built a transmitter and managed to send sound signals by radio waves. A year later, he built a more powerful transmitter and a receiver. He sent a signal from his garden to a field 1½ miles away.

Marconi offered his invention to the Italian Ministry of Posts and Telegraphs. To his great disappointment, they turned his idea down. He went to London, where he demonstrated his invention to officials from the Post Office. They were impressed and told the British Government about Marconi.

Marconi was asked to give a demonstration to

army and navy officers on Salisbury Plain. The navy was interested in using wireless telegraphy for shipping. Marconi sent a message across the English Channel in 1899 and across the Atlantic in 1901, and his invention was universally adopted as an aid to shipping.

The human voice was first transmitted by radio in the US just before the First World War. By this time, Marconi had formed his own company. Although he was not very interested in radio for entertainment, his company continued to develop his invention. In 1920, the Marconi Company broadcast the first British radio program. People loved the idea. Six companies, including Marconi's, began to make wireless sets to cope with the demand. The first commercial radio station in the US began in Pittsburgh Bennsylvania in 1920, and in 1922, the British Broadcasting Company (BBC) was formed to broadcast regular programs in Great Britain.

Above *The young Marconi photographed with his "black box" – the first apparatus for telegraphy without wires.*

Below *Marconi sends a radio message across the English Channel in 1899.*

1874	born in Bologna, Italy
1894	begins to experiment with radio waves
1895	transmits a message to a field 1½ mi away
1896	successfully demonstrates his invention in London
1897	forms The Wireless Telegraph and Signal Company – later renamed Marconi's Wireless Telegraph Company
1899	sends a message across the English Channel
1901	sends a message across the Atlantic
1920	broadcasts first British radio program
1937	dies in Rome

15
John Logie Baird

One day in 1923, John Logie Baird was walking on the cliffs at Hastings in Sussex, England. The BBC had been founded the year before; and, as Baird walked, he began to think about radio. Suddenly, he had the idea of "seeing by wireless." By the end of his walk, Baird had worked out a way of transmitting pictures by wireless waves. This was the beginning of television.

Baird was the son of a Scottish minister. He qualified as an engineer, but hated the work. When he was twenty-six years old, he decided to give it up and try out some of his ideas for inventions. None of these were successful, and by the time he was thirty-five, he was penniless. Then, he had the idea that was to make him a celebrity overnight. He used old radio parts and other bits and pieces from scrap yards to try it

Below *Baird giving the first public demonstration of his invention, using a ventriloquist's dummy, in 1926.*

out. The clumsy contraption he made produced a flickering, shadowy picture on a white sheet behind it.

Baird borrowed money to improve his equipment, and rented an attic workshop in London. In 1926, he gave his first public demonstration, when he televised a ventriloquist's dummy. The demonstration was a great success, and, suddenly, Baird was famous. He set up a company and began to improve the quality of his pictures. In 1929, he persuaded the BBC to transmit a daily black-and-white service.

Meanwhile, two other British companies – the Marconi Company and Electrical Musical Instruments (EMI) – had started work on their own television system. In 1937, the BBC decided to adopt the Marconi-EMI system instead of the one invented by Baird. Baird, the pioneer of television, was ruined and remained sad and bitter until the day he died, nine years later.

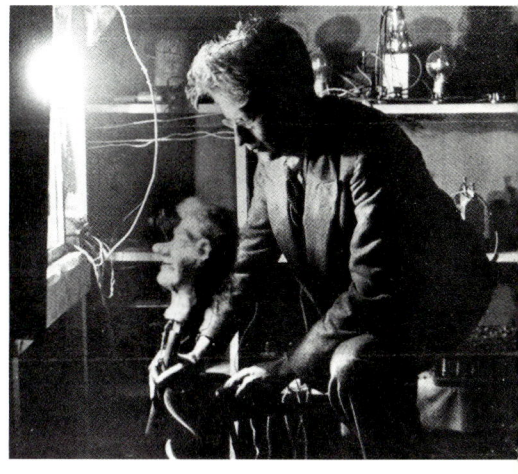

Above *Baird used many different pieces of equipment to make his television set.*

1888	born in Helensburgh, Scotland
1914	gives up career as engineer
1922	BBC founded
1923	begins work on television transmitter
1926	gives first public demonstration in his attic workshop in Soho, London
1928	demonstrates first color television
1929	begins daily black-and-white service using BBC transmitter
1937	BBC adopt Marconi-EMI system
1946	dies in Bexhill-on-Sea, Sussex, England

35

16
Caresse Crosby (Mary Phelps Jacob)

Nowadays, women can wear whatever kind of clothes they like. They can wear jeans or skirts, formal clothes or casual ones, and they can choose the colors and styles that suit them best. In earlier times, however, women were restricted in what they could wear. Until the First World War began in 1914, they wore long skirts which completely hid their legs. Their figures had to be "fashionable," too. Under their long dresses, they wore tightly-laced whalebone corsets which pulled in their waists and stomachs, pushed up their bosoms and gave them an "hourglass" figure.

In 1913, Mary Phelps Jacob was one of New York's leading debutantes, who went to two or three dances every night. She found it difficult

Caresse Crosby was an American debutante who loved dancing. She invented the brassiere to give herself and other women more freedom of movement.

to dance in the uncomfortable corsets which stretched from the armpits to the knees – a "box-like armor of whalebone," as she called them. She decided that she would not wear her corsets any more. Instead, she designed a brassiere (the word is French for a baby's undershirt). She made it from two handkerchiefs, which she sewed together and gathered along the seam. The garment was fastened at the back.

At first, people were shocked by this strange new idea, but women soon saw how much freedom of movement it gave them. More and more women were going out to work, and they needed practical, comfortable clothes. Blouses and skirts or suits began to replace tight dresses and corsets.

Mary Phelps Jacob married a millionaire called Harry Crosby and changed her name to Caresse. She lived to see many fashions come and go, but the brassiere has not changed a great deal since the day she invented it.

1892	born in the USA
1913	becomes one of New York's leading debutantes; designs the first brassiere
1970	dies in the USA

17
Ladislao Biro

You may never have heard of Ladislao Biro, but you have certainly heard of the writing implement he invented – the ball-point pen. Before Biro invented his pen, people wrote with fountain pens. The ink smudged and blotted, and the pens sometimes leaked. In the 1930s Biro was a magazine editor in Budapest, Hungary. He noticed that the inks which the magazine's printers used dried very quickly. Biro wondered if quick-drying inks could be used in pens. He came up with the idea of a tube of ink with a free-moving ball on the end. As a person wrote, the ball collected ink from the tube and rolled it onto the paper. The pen would be cheap and could be thrown away when the ink ran out.

Biro began to work on his invention, but before he could patent it, the Second World War broke out. Biro left war-torn Europe and fled to Buenos Aires in Argentina. There, he and his brother Georg, who was a chemist, began to improve the pen. In the early 1940s, Biro began to manufacture his new pen, the biro.

Biro did not have enough money to start a big manufacturing company. In 1944, he sold his invention to another company, who began to mass-produce the pen for the British and American armed forces. The servicemen and women liked the pens because they did not leak and were easy to carry around.

Biro was pleased that his pen was popular, but he did not gain much from his invention. The biro was later sold to the French firm, Bic, who now sell twelve million pens a day. Biro sank into obscurity in South America, and it is not known whether he is still alive today.

1900	born in Hungary
1938	applies for patent for first ball-point pen
1939	flees from Hungary to escape Nazis; goes to France, Spain and then Argentina
c. 1943	begins to manufacture pens
1944	sells invention

Biro's ball-point pen became popular with servicemen and women as well as with schoolchildren.

18
Sir Frank Whittle

Modern airplanes are powered by jet engines. They can reach great heights and travel at very fast speeds. The jet engine was pioneered by an English pilot and engineer, Frank Whittle.

Frank Whittle joined the Royal Air Force (RAF) in 1923, and later became a fighter pilot. At this time, all airplanes were driven by propellers turned by piston engines, which worked in the same way as a car engine. The planes could not fly at very high altitudes or at very fast speeds. While he was in the RAF, Whittle came up with a better idea: to thrust an aircraft forward with a powerful backward jet of gas. Air would be drawn in at the front of the engine and compressed by a rotary fan, or compressor. This fan would be driven by a gas turbine at the back. The compressed air would be mixed with kerosene and ignited. This would cause the air to expand and rush out through the turbine, making it spin to drive the compressor. The hot gases would then be forced out through a nozzle at the back of the engine, thrusting the aircraft forward.

Below *The Gloster Meteor, powered by Whittle's jet engine, attacking a flying bomb (V1) during the Second World War.*

Whittle patented his idea in 1930. He needed more technical knowledge before he could develop it fully, so he studied at Cambridge University for three years. Then he set up a company to build jet engines. His first engine, the *Whittle W1*, was tested in 1937. In 1941, the *Gloster E28/39* airplane, powered by the Whittle engine, made its first flight. But it was not the first jet flight of all. A German, Hans von Ohain, had already achieved jet flight in 1939, and his jet fighter, the *Messerschmitt 262*, entered the Second World War in 1944.

Whittle's invention was not used until almost the end of the war, when the *Gloster Meteor* jet went into action. After the war, the jet engine was developed for commercial airplanes. The first British jet airliner was built in 1949.

When this book was published, Sir Frank Whittle was living in quiet retirement in England.

1907	born in Coventry, England
1923	joins RAF
1926	becomes an Officer Cadet at the RAF College at Cranwell
1930	patents jet engine
1937	*Whittle W1* tested on the ground
1941	first flight of *Gloster E28/39* powered by a Whittle engine
1945	*Gloster Meteor* jet goes into action in the Second World War
1948	retires from RAF as an Air Commodore; knighted for his work
1948–52	honorary Technical Advisor, Jet Development, for British Overseas Airways Corporation (BOAC)

19
Wernher Von Braun

On July 20, 1969, two American astronauts, Neil Armstrong and Edwin "Buzz" Aldrin, climbed out of *Apollo 11's* landing unit *Eagle* and walked on the moon. The first landing of men on the moon was one of the most spectacular achievements the world has seen, and the man behind it was a German engineer, Wernher von Braun.

Von Braun was studying engineering in Berlin when he read an article by a German scientist, Hermann Oberth, about sending rockets into space. Von Braun vowed that he would build a rocket to send men to the moon. He began to develop rockets in a rented warehouse at Kummersdorf, near Berlin. In 1937, he was made the technical director of the German army's rocket station on the Baltic coast.

During the Second World War, von Braun designed secret rockets for Germany. In 1944, his first long-range rocket weapon, the *V2*, was launched against Britain and France, causing many deaths. In 1945, von Braun and his team of engineers took the *V2* plans and surrendered themselves to the American forces.

The V2, *von Braun's first long-range rocket, was launched in 1944.*

- **1912** born in Wirsitz, Germany
- **1932** begins building and testing rockets at Kummersdorf, near Berlin
- **1937** becomes technical director of German army's rocket station at Peenemünde on the Baltic Coast
- **1944** first *V2* rockets launched against Britain and France
- **1945** escapes from Peenemünde and surrenders to US forces
- **1957** Russians launch *Sputnik 1*
- **1959** Russians launch first man, Yuri Gagarin, into space
- **1969** *Saturn V* launched on its journey to the moon, Neil Armstrong and Edwin Aldrin land on the moon
- **1977** dies in Alexandria, Virginia

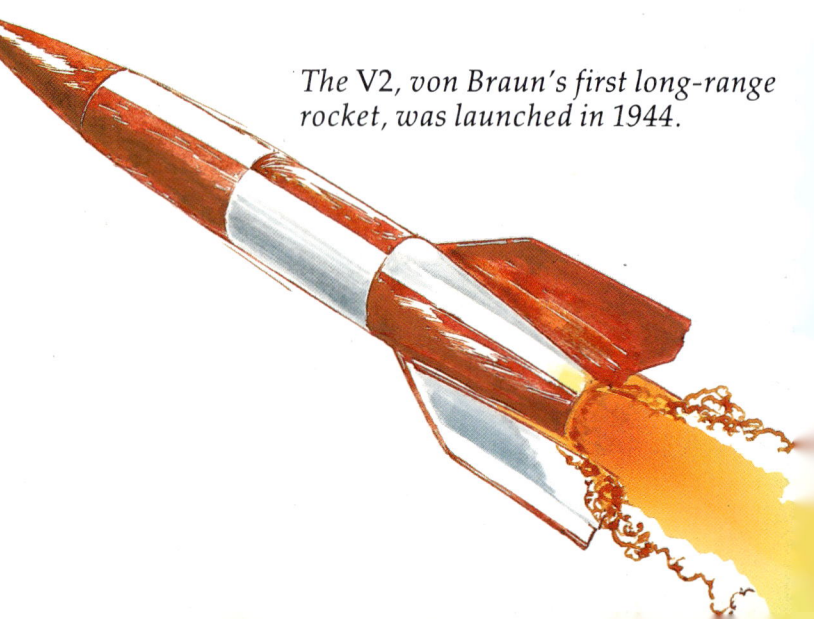

After the war, the German team went to the US. At first, von Braun worked on military weapons. Then, in 1957, the Russians launched their unmanned satellite, *Sputnik 1*, into space. Von Braun persuaded the United States government to let him build space rockets for them. The government set up a new space center at Houston, Texas, with von Braun as its director.

No one had by then built a rocket with a long enough range to reach outer space – and the moon. Von Braun and his team designed a rocket with three sections. The tail launched the rocket, then fell away. The middle section surged on until it also burned up. Finally, the nose section holding the spacecraft, fell away, leaving the spacecraft to travel on alone. It was in this rocket, the *Saturn 5*, with its spacecraft *Apollo 11*, that the American astronauts reached the moon in 1969.

Von Braun and his team designed the rocket Saturn 5 *with its spacecraft* Apollo 11, *in which men first landed on the moon.*

20
Rosalind Franklin

Why do you look the way you do? Why are different characteristics handed down from parent to child, generation after generation? For thousands of years, no one knew the answers to these questions. In 1865, a monk named Gregor Mendel discovered a pattern in the way characteristics are inherited. Nearly a century later, scientists discovered a substance called DNA (deoxyribonucleic acid). They learned that heredity works because the necessary genetic information is stored and passed on by the DNA molecules contained in all living things. The structure of the DNA molecule was officially discovered in 1953 by two scientists, James Watson and Francis Crick, but much of the research which made their discovery possible was carried out by a young scientist named Rosalind Franklin.

Rosalind Franklin realized that she wanted to be a scientist while she was at St. Paul's Girls'

Rosalind Franklin's research played a vital part in the discovery in 1953 of the DNA molecule which determines hereditary characteristics.

School in London, England. After four years at Cambridge University, she became a research officer at the British Coal Utilization Research Association, and, in 1947, went to Paris as a laboratory researcher. It was here that she learned the techniques which carried her into her work with DNA. She used these techniques to study the structure of minerals, but felt that they were also suitable for examining biological substances.

In 1950, Rosalind returned to England to work on DNA at King's College, London. As the work progressed, she discussed it with other scientists and gave lectures on the subject. She did not realize that Watson and Crick, who were studying DNA at Cambridge, were racing her for the answer. In 1953, Watson and Crick won the race, but Rosalind Franklin's earlier discoveries played a crucial part in the final result.

Rosalind Franklin died of cancer when she was only thirty-seven. The contribution she had made to science was enormous.

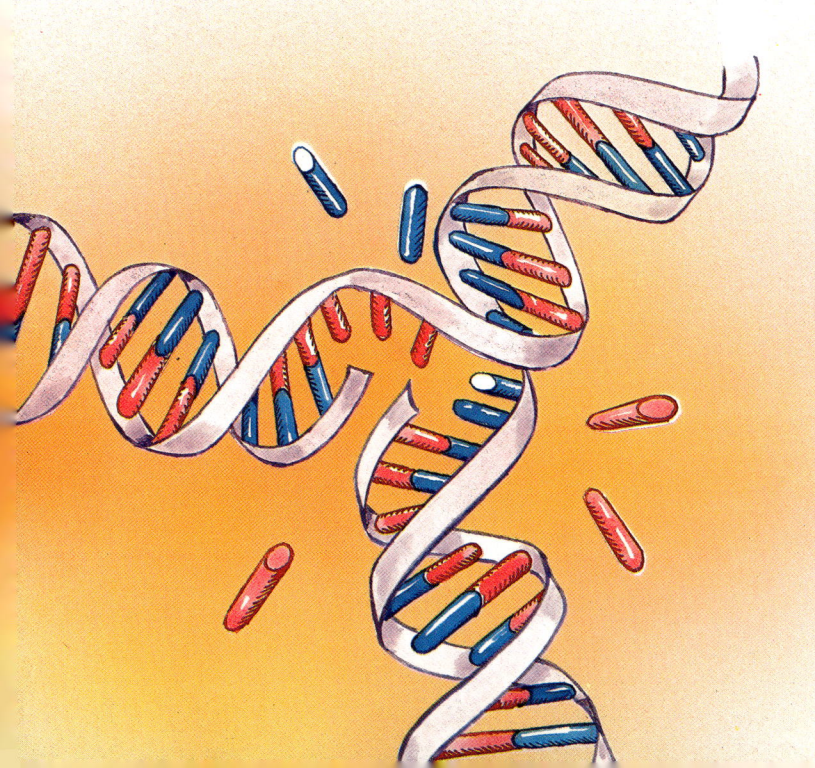

1920	born in London, England
1938–41	studies science at Cambridge University
1941	presented with research scholarship by Newnham College
1942	leaves Cambridge to work as assistant research officer at the British Coal Utilization Research Association (CURA)
1947	goes to Paris as researcher at the Laboratoire Central des Services Chimiques de l'Etat
1952	lectures and prepares report of her experiments and discoveries about the DNA molecule
1953	Watson and Crick present their solution to the DNA problem; moves to Birkbeck College, London, where she spends the rest of her life working on viruses
1958	dies of cancer in London

Glossary

Atom Smallest particle in any element.
Biplane A plane with two sets of wings, one above the other.
Carbon A chemical element. Diamonds are one form of carbon, and partly burned wood, or charcoal, is another.
Compress To squeeze into a small space.
Condense When warm water vapor (steam) is cooled down quickly and turns into water.
Cylinder The part of an engine where the piston is forced back and forth by steam or by burning fuel.
Elements The basic chemical ingredients from which every substance on earth is made.
Filament The fine wire in an electric light bulb, which gives off light when heated by an electric current.
Genetic Concerning the genes, or parts of the cells which govern heredity.
Heredity The passing of characteristics such as the color of eyes and hair, or shape of features, from parent to child.
Internal combustion engine An engine which is driven by burning fuel inside a cylinder, forcing a piston to move back and forth to drive the moving parts of the machinery.
Molecule Two or more atoms joined together.
Nobel Prize The highest award for achievement in a particular field of science or art.
Patent A government permit which insures that the inventor is the only person who can make or sell his or her invention.
Pneumatic Something which is filled with, or driven by, air.
Radioactive A word used to describe a substance that gives off powerful rays which can penetrate solid material such as metal, glass or the human body.
Receiver A device for picking up sound or radio waves, such as a radio or television set or a telephone receiver.
Sophisticated More complex and efficient.
Telegraph A way of sending messages along wires by electricity.
Transmitter A device for sending out sound or radio waves.
Tuberculosis A disease contracted by breathing in contaminated air. It affects various parts of the body including the lungs.
Tumor Swelling or growth in the body.
Turbine A wheel which is made to spin very fast by a powerful flow of water or by a jet of steam or expanding hot air.
Uranium A radioactive mineral used to produce nuclear power found in certain parts of the world, including Australia, Canada and the US.
Waves Light, heat and radio waves are all types of radiation – rays which travel through space at very high speeds.

Further reading

Dreamers and Doers: Inventors Who Changed the World by Norman Richards (Macmillan, 1984)
Growing Up with Science: The Illustrated Encyclopedia of Invention edited by Michael Dempsey (Stuttman, 1987)
How to Be an Inventor by Harvey Weiss (Harper & Row Junior Books, 1980)
Inventions No One Mentions by Chip Lovitt (Scholastic, 1987)
The Inventors: Nobel Prizes in Chemistry, Physics and Medicine by Nathan Aaseng (Lerner, 1987)
Marie Curie: Brave Scientist by Keith Brandt (Troll Associates, 1983)
One Thousand Inventions by Alan Benjamin (Macmillan, 1980)
Small Inventions That Make a Big Difference edited by Donald J. Crump (National Geographic Society, 1984)
The Story of Thomas Alva Edison by Margaret Cousins (Random House, 1981)
The Unconventional Invention Book by Bob Stanish (Good Apple, 1981)

Index

Airplanes 31, 40, 41
Aldrin, Edwin 42
American War Department 31
Apollo 11 42, 43
Archimedes 6–7
Archimedes' Principle 7
Archimedes' Screw 6
Argentina 39
Arkwright, Richard 10–11
Armitage, Dr. 17
Armstrong, Neil 42
Astronauts 42, 43
Atlantic Ocean 33
Automobile 20, 21, 23

Baird, John Logie 34–5
Ball-point pen 38
Barbier, Captain Charles 17
Bell, Alexander Graham 5, 24–5
Bicycle 21, 22
Berlin 42
Biro, Ladislao 38–9
Blind people 16
Bologna, Italy 32
Books 8
Boston, Massachusetts 24, 25
Boulton, Matthew 13
Braille alphabet 16, 17
Braille, Louis 16–17
Brassiere 37
British Broadcasting Company (BBC) 33, 34, 35
British Coal Utilization Research Association 45
British government 32
Burt, William 18
Businesses 19

Cambridge University 41, 45
Canada 24
Cancer 29, 45
Canstatt 21
Canvas 23
Carbon filament 27

Catapults 7
Coal mines 12, 14
Compressor 40
Cotton weavers 11
Crick, Francis 44, 45
Crosby, Caresse 36–7
Curie, Marie 28–9
Curie, Pierre 28, 29

Daimler, Gottlieb 20–21
Daimler Motor Company 21
Deaf children 24
Debutantes 37
Detroit, Michigan 18
DNA molecules 5, 44, 45
Dunlop, John 22–3
Dunlop Rubber Company 23

Eagle 42
Edison Electric Light Company 27
Edison, Thomas Alva 26–7
Electric current 27
Electrical Musical Instruments (EMI) 35
Electricity 26, 27, 32
Electric light 26, 27
Engineer 14, 15, 34, 40, 42
Euclid 6

Farming 4
Faraday, Michael 26
First World War 33, 36
Flyer 30, 31
Fountain pen 38
France 16, 31, 42
Franklin, Rosalind 5, 44–5
Fust, Johann 9

Gasoline 20
Gas turbine 40
Genetic information 44
Geometry 6
Germany 21, 42
Glasgow University 12
Glidden, Carlos 18, 19

Glider 30
Gloster E28/39 41
Gloster Meteor 41
Gold Indicator Company 26
Goldsmiths 8
Gutenberg Bible 9
Gutenberg, Johann 5, 8–9

Hancock, Thomas 22
Hargreaves, James 10
Heredity 44
Hieron, King of Syracuse 7
"Horseless carriage" 20, 21
Horsepower 13, 30
Hot-air balloon 30
Hungary 38

Internal combustion engine 20, 30
Iron 22
Italian Ministry of Posts and Telegraphs 32

Jeans 36
Jellinek, Emil 21
Jet airliner 41
Jet engines 40, 41
Jewelry 4

Laboratory 29
Lenoir, Etienne 20
"Letter printing machine" 18
Libraries 8
Life on the Mississippi 19
Light bulb 27
Lillienthal, Otto 30
Linen 11
Liverpool, England 15
Locomotion 15

Magazines 8, 38
Magnetic waves 32
Mainz, Germany 8
Manchester, England 15
Marcellus, General 7
Marconi Company 33, 35

47

Marconi, Guglielmo 32–3
Mathematics 28
Mendel, Gregor 44
Menlo Park, New York 26, 27
Mercedes 21
Messerschmitt 262 41
Military planes 31, 40, 41
Miller, Henry 18
Minerals 4, 28, 45
Milwaukee 18
Model 1 Remington 19
Montgolfier brothers 30
Moon, landing on 42
Motorcycle 21
Motor industry 20

National Institute for Blind Youth 16, 17
Newcomen engine 12, 13
Newcomen, Thomas 12
New Jersey 26
Newspapers 8, 18, 31, 32
New York 26, 27, 37
"Night writing" 17
North Carolina 31
Northern Ireland 23

Oberth, Hermann 42
Ohio 30
Ornaments 4
Otto, Nikolaus 20, 21
Outer space 43

Paris 16, 28, 30, 45
Phelps Jacob, Mary (see Crosby, Caress)
Phonograph 26, 27
Physics 28
Piston engines 40
Pitchblende 28, 29

Pneumatic tire 22
Polonium 29
Printing press 5, 8, 9
Propellers 40

Quick-drying inks 38

Radioactivity 28, 29, 46
Radio waves 32
Radium 29
Railroad 15
Receiver
  radio 32
  telephone 25
Remington Small Arms Company 19
Rocket 15
Rockets 42, 43
Rubber
  air-filled inner tubes 23
  tires 22, 23

Saturn 5 43
Scotland 12, 24
Second World War 39, 41, 42
Scholes, Christopher 18–19
Sorbonne, University of Paris 28
Soulé, Samuel 19
Sound waves 24
Spacecraft 43
Spinning 10
  jenny 10
  mill 11
  water powered frame 10, 11
  wheels 10
Sputnik 1 43
Steam engine 5, 12, 13, 14
Steam locomotive 14
Stephenson, George 14–15

Stephenson, Robert 14
Stockton and Darlington Railway 14

Telegrams 24
Television 34, 35
Telephone 5, 24, 25
Texas 43
Thomson, Robert William 22
Tools 4
Transmitter
  radio 32
  telephone 25, 26
Trevithick, Richard 14
Tricycle 23
Twain, Mark 19
Typewriter 18, 19
Typographer 18

United States government 43
Uranium 28, 29, 46

V2 42
Ventriloquist's dummy 34
Vibrating disc 25
Von Braun, Wernher 42–3
Von Ohain, Hans 41

Warsaw 28
Watson, James 44, 45
Watson, Thomas 25
Watt, James 5, 12–13
Whalebone corsets 36, 37
Whittle, Sir Frank 40–41
Whittle W1 41
Wireless telegraphy 33
Wireless waves 34
Women inventors 5, 28
Wright brothers 30–31

Picture acknowledgements

Mary Evans Picture Library 13, 29, 35; Peter Newark's Western Americana 21, 33; Ann Ronan Picture Library 11, 19, 25, 27; Wayland Picture Library 9.